30 DAY PERSONAL PRAYER REVIVAL

A 30 Day Journey That Will Transform Your Life From Stagnation To Acceleration!

LaShele N. Jones-Evans

Copyright © 2017 by It's Milan's Theory Publishing Company. All rights reserved. No part of this book may be reproduced in any form without permission from the author, except by reviewer who may quote passages to be printed in a newspaper or magazine.

Liberty of Congress Control Number: In publication data

ISBN: 978-0-999-1590-4-0

30 Day Personal Prayer Revival

Author: LaShele N. Jones-Evans

Cover & Back Design: www.fiverr.com/magicdesignx & www.fiverr.com/Amjed_viera

Editor: LaKeisha McKenzie

Interior Design: www.fiverr.com/kindlequeen

Published by: LaShele N. Jones-Evans

DEDICATIONS

This book is dedicated to the following:

My first love, "MyDad" Noah P. Brown-Wilkerson. You taught me the importance of family and being selfless. Because of you I somehow think I can feed a whole community with 2 fish and 5 loaves of bread (lol) Your heart was so big! I know you're watching over me and I hope you're proud of the woman I've become! I LOVE & MISS YOU!

My mother-in-love, Joan Evans. Thank you for accepting me as your daughter and assisting me with raising my children. Your strong, independent personality taught me how to make it through some of the toughest obstacles in life. I APPRECIATE YOUR LOVE! REST WELL MRS. J!

My spiritual father, Nathaniel "Mickey" Henry. Your wisdom and knowledge assisted in my growth as a leader for the Kingdom of God. Our talks are embedded in my heart forever. They still guide me to this day! THANK YOU! REST IN PARADISE!

ACKNOWLEDGEMENTS

All glory and honor goes to God. Without Him, nothing would be possible.

A special thank you to K.D. Harris, founder of The Purposed Pen Project. Thank you for your patience and expertise with assisting me getting my first book completed.

To the love of my life, my husband, Damion D. Evans Sr. Thanks for giving up some of "our" time so I could focus on completing this project. You were my strength throughout this entire process. You have been my coach, my drill sergeant and my #1 cheerleader. Your input on days 4 and 27 were challenging to say the least (lol), but you pushed me beyond mediocre. THANKS FOR BELIEVING IN MY POTENTIAL.

To my children, Myesha, Alonzo, Tae, Damiah, Boo-Boo and Dai-Dai. Thanks for constantly keeping me on my face in prayer (lol) You guys are wonderful children and have been instrumental in my growth as a mother and prayer warrior. Y'all support means everything to me. To my grandchildren; Milan Auriel and Theory Chanel, and my God-children (Lonja, TreNae, Corynn, Damarion & King) because of y'all, I don't quit. Y'all are my inspiration. Everything I do is to leave a legacy to you. To my God-given bonus children Ciara Smallwood, Lynnette Thomas & Tharron "Caddy" Shehee, thank you for allowing me to be a part of your life.

To my awesome mother, Leslie A. Jones-Wilkerson, who deserves endless thanks. You have taught me how to be a strong, persevering woman. Those characteristics have enabled me to carry this vision to completion. YOU ARE MY EVERYTHING!

To my siblings; Omega Lamane, Tiffany Noel, Noah Preston and Leslie May. Thank y'all for being my first best friends. ***"Chilly's kids"*** To my sister's/brother in love: Herb, Hope, Shinda & my Teen Bean (Chrissy) I love and appreciate you guys.

To the best church in the universe! Heaven Touched Outreach Ministry. I always say I Pastor some of the greatest people on this side of heaven. Thank you for entrusting me with your spiritual lives and thank you for always having my back.

Special Thanks: Donnail and Toni Lister, Terance and Artisha Hall, Neimon and Tish Barbour, David and Cheryl Brown, Banzina Pressey, Pamela McCarthney-Caldwell, Rosalind Williams, Vianca Black, Rita Clark and Leonette Collins. You guys have been consistent and motivators in my life. Your support has been astronomical and I appreciate you!

To my forever spiritual mother; Apostle Linda Henry. It was you that raised me in the Gospel. I'm forever grateful and thankful for your nurturing, teaching and directions. You taught me the importance, the power and purpose of prayer. Thank you!

Shout out to my spiritual little sisters (Keisha McKenzie, JeNae Henderson, Keona Robinson & Jhonita "Toodie" Ervin) y'all have been a major blessing to my life. Thanks for loving me (almost) as must as I love y'all!

30 Day Personal Prayer Revival

Through prayer we gain insight and access to heavenly tools that help reflect God's character and His Kingdom! Let's fold our hands, bend our knees, compose our minds, expecting a personal change that will equip and provoke us not only to become better but to change the world!

...Through Prayer!

Introduction

The purpose of this 30 day journey is to ignite and restore your zeal for Christ. This journey will challenge you to pray boldly and consistently for every area of your life. We've given you room to write down your thoughts and reflect on what you've read. Keep in mind that you are just beginning this journey of restoration. You will be in an ongoing process of learning and discovering the power of your identity through prayer for the rest of your life. He is the One who will guide you through this exciting journey.

As you embark on this journey to reignite your life, I pray that God would open you up to who you truly are in Him. I want to encourage you to be committed to praying every day for the next 30 days. This journey will take you through emptying out what doesn't belong and fill you up with what you need (God's character, desires and will). I believe 30 days from now your life will go from stagnated to accelerated!

I recommend you go through this journey for 30 days straight first. After the first 30 days is completed feel free to choose random days to read and pray. You may also find yourself doing this 30 day journey more than once! Get what you need as often as you need it!

Table of Contents

Dedications I
Acknowledgements II
Introduction V
The Lord's Prayer 1
Day 1: A New Day, A New Me! Cleanse Me 3
Day 2: Show Me, Me 7
Day 3: Empty Me 11
Day 4: Build Me Up 15
Day 5: No Request - Grateful For Grace 20
Day 6: Intercession 23
Day 7: Renew My Mind 27
Day 8: Ask, Seek, Knock 32
Day 9: Restoration 36
Day 10: Encourage Yourself 41
Day 11: Protection 43
Day 12: Declaring 47
Day 13: Covered 52
Day 14: Casting Down 56
Day 15: Value Vision 61
Day 16: Transform 64
Day 17: Breathe 68
Day 18: Reveal 72
Day 19: Lead My Seed 76

Day 20: Show Mercy 80
Day 21: Surrender 84
Day 22: Your Personal Day 88
Day 23: Position Me 90
Day 24: Prepared 94
Day 25: No Request - Thankful For Grace & Mercy ... 98
Day 26: Serpent Wisdom 101
Day 27: Humility 105
Day 28: Fasting & Meditating 109
Day 29: Endurance 113
Day 30: Praise - It's Always In Order 116

The Lord's Prayer

{Matthew 6:9-13 Kjv}
In this manner, therefore, pray:

Our Father in heaven,

Hallowed be Your name.

Your kingdom come.

Your will be done

On earth as it is in heaven.

Give us this day our daily bread.

And forgive us our debts,

As we forgive our debtors.

And do not lead us into temptation,

But deliver us from the evil one.

For Yours is the kingdom and the power and the glory forever. Amen.

When Jesus' disciples asked Him to teach them how to pray, Jesus responded by giving them a fixed prayer to recite {Matt 6:9-13}. In that prayer, He taught them what they most needed to ask of God. As they prayed it attentively, He knew that their hearts and will would be changed and brought more and more in line with what they were asking of God. What they were seeking in prayer was fully attuned to the change that God wanted to bring about in them and the direction in which God wanted them to go.

DAY 1

"A NEW DAY, A NEW ME! CLEANSE ME"

Cleansing starts with being honest, "I AM UNCLEAN" Romans 3:23 (Kjv) "for all have sinned and fall short of the glory of God." And we must then acknowledge "WHAT IS MAKING US UNCLEAN" From unclean to clean starts with REPENTING. The beginning of doing a new thing is turning from the old.

As a child I remember attending First Baptist Church, sitting in a Sunday school class listening to the teacher teach on sin. He taught us that when we go to God in prayer if we don't ask God to forgive us, then a BIG block of sin would separate us and we wouldn't be able to talk to Him. Being about 10 years old that image horrified me and has sort of stuck with me into adulthood. I understand unrepentance keeps us separate from Him. In Mark 15:34 while on the cross, Christ called out, "My God, My God, why have You forsaken Me?" It was the sins of the world that Christ took on for the sake of salvation that caused God to turn away from His son (for a moment). This moment reflects the burden of sin and abandonment by God because of it. As believers of Christ that have a desire to be all that He willed us to be, we must live a life of repentance. Repenting daily keeps our hearts and hands clean before God. Sin is against the nature of God and that is why God always commands everyone, everywhere to repent. Acts 17:30 "Truly, these times of ignorance God overlooked, but now commands all men everywhere to repent." As you travel this 30 day journey of prayer, *repenting ought to be in the forefront of each prayer.* Repenting is not only confessing your sins to God but is also turning from your old you and embracing the new you! DAILY!

Scripture: {Psalm 51:1-11 Nkjv} Have mercy upon me, O God, According to Your loving kindness; According to the multitude of Your tender mercies, Blot out my transgressions. Wash me thoroughly from my iniquity, And cleanse me from my sin. For I acknowledge my transgressions, And my sin *is* always before me. Against You, You only, have I sinned, And done *this* evil in Your sight—That You may be found just when You speak, *And* blameless when You judge. Behold, I was brought forth in iniquity, And in sin my mother conceived me. Behold, You desire truth in the inward parts, And in the hidden *part* You will make me to know wisdom. Purge me with hyssop, and I shall be clean; Wash me, and I shall be whiter than snow. Make me hear joy and gladness That the bones You have broken may rejoice. Hide Your face from my sins, And blot out all my iniquities. *Create in me a clean heart, O God, And renew a steadfast spirit within me.* Do not cast me away from Your presence, And do not take Your Holy Spirit from me.

Prayer: *Father I acknowledge I am unclean. Forgive me for my sins committed against you! The sins of my actions, my thoughts and my words! (Be specific about these sins) Father forgives me for my sins against my brothers and sisters! (Be specific about these sins) Father, forgive me for things that are in my heart that cause me to sin against you. Cleanse me thoroughly of* *my iniquity, cleanse me of my sins. Father, make me aware (convict me) of known, unknown and unintentional sin and forgive me! Create in me a new heart and new mind while teaching me your ways that I would sin against you no more.*

DAY 2

"SHOW ME, ME"

...The Good, The Bad & The Ugly

Prepare your heart & mind to see the real you! The you that is GREAT in God but limited because of some not so great things that are in you! As I took this prayer revival journey myself, I discovered some ways in me, I considered "justifiable" were a hindrance to my growth in God. It wasn't until I went before the Lord and asked, "GOD why am I still in the same condition? I've prayed for the constant change but things are still the same." God showed me how what was in me, hindered me! I learned to stop praying for the hearts and eyes of others and I first prayed for my own. As God continues to revive and replenish you, you must allow God to open your eyes to you. God has created an extraordinary masterpiece; YOU! *The GOOD*: See the "fearfully & wonderfully" made you that David talked about in Psalm 139:14. David was in awe of God's handiwork; himself. As you too should be in awe of the you God created. Understand everything God created was good, including YOU! It's important to seek God for the great things IN you. Be excited about those things by giving God thanks and doing your best with those things. Discover your identity in Christ and stand in it confidently. Unfortunately, you only discover the good when you rid the bad. *The BAD*: Satan uses this to keep your identity hidden. When you believe you're nothing, you do nothing! When you believe you're a failure, you fail! When you settle for less, you never go beyond your limits. The good in you is never exposed or manifested because it's being hidden or pushed to the back by the bad. The bad hinders you from being effective. And then there's the ugly. *The UGLY*: Our make up or our reactions. Unlike the bad, the ugly isn't the act of Satan, it's what you do as a reaction to the bad. You ever felt like a failure so you don't apply yourself to anything? So you make no efforts to use your gifts, power or purpose to be successful. What you don't do becomes your make-up; the ugly. Because of our fleshly nature, we must constantly do a self-check. Acknowledge and honor who God intended you to be. If you're not quite sure yet, take inventory of your life. Acknowledge the good (no matter how small you think it is) and give God thanks for that. Ask God to show you how to be confident with what/who you are. (List some of the things in you that you know are great; character traits, gifts, abilities, etc) You must also be willing to rid that which is unpleasing to God. It is important. Be willing to do whatever's necessary to rid yourself of the bad and the ugly so your good can SHINE!

Scripture: {Romans 7:17-20 Msg} But I need something more! For if I know the law but still can't keep it, and if the power of sin within me keeps sabotaging my best intentions, I obviously need help! I realize that I don't have what it takes. I can will it, but I can't do it. I decide to do good, but I don't really do it; I decide not to do bad, but then I do it anyway. My decisions, such as they are, don't result in actions. Something has gone wrong deep within me and gets the better of me every time.

Prayer: *Dear Lord, Show me, me! Help me to be confident and courageous in who you created me to be. Allow me to see the knowledge of your will that your Spirit gives, so that I may live a life worthy of you. Expose every broken place & every place of hindrance to me. Show me how to stand in who called me to be that deliverance will truly be my portion. Open my eyes to the adversary that keeps me blinded. Open my eyes to all power of darkness that have been set to stop my purpose and open my eyes to the power of You that work in me. My desire is to bear fruit in every good work, growing in the knowledge of You, being strengthened and empowered according to your might. (List every good thing that you recognize about yourself. Remember it doesn't matter how small you may think it is. Allow the good things to overthrow any bad or ugly. Ex: Lord thank you for the the love I have in my heart that will drive out any bitterness. Lord allow the creativity of my mind to drive out any stagnation and my desire to succeed drive out any laziness.)*

DAY 3

"EMPTY ME"

...Fill Me Up With Your Spirit!

This is the time for declutter! When you are full of distractions, burdens and anxiety to name a few, you hinder your effectiveness in GOD. Just living life sometimes consumes you. Family, bills, careers and goal pursuits are not necessarily bad things; they are a part of life. But when you're trying to manage it all, it can become consuming which often times lead to "burdensome." It's important to ask God to empty you of things that hinder you from "seeking" first the Kingdom. I noticed a lot of times I waited until I was completely full with stuff; worry, weariness, overwhelmed, etc. before I would start trying to "empty". When filling a bathtub, if you don't empty it of water, it will continue to fill until it overflows. When it overflows, because of what's in it (water) it could damage your floors! Don't wait until the clutter in you is spilling over and its causes a negative effect in your life or the lives of others. Empty now, before it becomes too much. My husband would often tell me, "You're spreading yourself thin. You're making yourself too available to others and not taking care of you! You're trying to make everything happen and you're only one person" I would argue with him because clearly, Philippians 4:13 says, "I can do all things through Christ who strengthens me" right? But what happens when you're trying to fulfill purpose out of order? When you're trying to do all things but not strategically. The key to success is following God's plans for our lives as He designed and/or ordered it. Anything out of order causes confusion. Confusion is one of our greatest opponents in life. When you're confused, you're out of place with no sense of direction. It wasn't until I realized I was doing a lot of everything and nothing was getting completed. I was out of place in my life and promises, fulfillment, peace & joy were not my portions. I'd go to bed with so much on my mind, worrying about things I truly had no control over! Matthew 6:34 teaches us not to worry about tomorrow because tomorrow will take care of itself. Don't anticipate tomorrow's outcome when your thoughts are negative or all over the place! That could possibly take away from today's strength, strategy and peace that are setting you up for tomorrow! We all need to be emptied of things that hinder us from hearing God, obeying God and enjoying God! Often times we think sin is our only hindrance in being effective but the way we handle life could also be a hindrance. Today you want to pray that you're emptied of all sin as well as chaos, confusion and conflict. As you're being emptied it's important to invite and make space available for God and all His attributes. As God begins to occupy space in your mind and your heart, tomorrow won't be an issue of your mind it will become a goal, desire or a "seeking" of God's order for your life. We can accumulate sin, chaos, confusion and conflict in our lives that hinder our ability to be used by God. To be used we must be emptied and available! When all of you is out of the way, all of God can come in and do His will.

Scripture: {Romans 15:13 Nkjv} Now may the God of hope fill you with all joy and peace in believing, that you may abound in hope by the power of the Holy Spirit.

Prayer: *Lord, I come to you full of much that clutters, distracts, stifles and burdens me! My desire is to emptied of (be specific) self-dissatisfactions, wasteful preoccupations of my heart and mind. Empty me of the ways I consider myself powerless, a victim, being less than I am or as other than yours. Fill my life with order, a whole heart, holiness, confidence in you, joy, peace, strategies & resources. My desire is for an abundant life! A kingdom life! As you empty me of what doesn't belong, fill every empty place of you! Fill my eyes with your vision, fill my ears with your voice and fill my heart and mouth with your word!*

DAY 4

"BUILD ME UP"

...Strengthen me where I'm weak, provoke me where I'm (s)lacking that I may also build others effectively.

It is very important that our minds be renewed through the knowledge of God's Word, giving us a clear understanding of God's perspective of our weakness. It is often through weakness God proves His strength. When our lives run smoothly we have a tendency to rely on our human strength. Strength that in no way can compare to the strength of Christ. However when life besets us and becomes challenging at times our human strength fades quickly and we become weak. In these times of personal weakness, God shows Himself invincible and faithful!

My dad always taught us to look out for the less fortunate. My dad was always feeding the community, having events and gatherings for everyone he came in contact with. Because of that upbringing I always enjoyed helping others. I always imagined opening up a facility that would feed & clothe people as well as help them get jobs to do better in life. Well in 2014, the Lord called me to Pastor my own church. Because it was already instilled in me before I came to know the Lord, my desire was to help people with life. Never did I imagine it would be on a "Pastoral" level. So my testimony wasn't "I ran from the call" and "God made me do it." I was humbled and excited to be used; even after serving in a church for a little over 10 years watching the hardships of my Pastor. I often witnessed her at some of her weakest moments while pastoring but I always took note of God's continuous strength given to her. She too found joy in serving others. Soon after I stepped into the Pastor role I started having Bible Studies in a community center until an affordable building became available. One night, I found myself in the emergency room with chest pains. After many test, doctors couldn't figure out what was wrong. They only knew fluid was surrounding my lungs and they had no idea where it was coming from. I had to have surgery and drainage tubes. After the procedure, I had to have monthly checks up to find out where this fluid came from...no answers! I was finally told by my doctor that she has seen this in others and their life expectancy was about 18 months. I had to go through countless tests, scans and MRI's and it was taking a toll on my body. The physical trauma was only a small portion of my despair! My mental and spiritual state suffered most! As I fought hard to believe God for healing, I felt weak! Spiritually drained. This situation had zapped my strength! Fear and the unknown had taken my confidence! Everything in me wanted to step away from Pastoring but I just couldn't. By this time I had a few members that were depending on me serving them and many had sown into the ministry. So I continued on for the sake of others but within, I was the weakest spiritually, I had ever been. In the midst of me trying to be what the people needed and what I thought God expected of me I was losing myself! In all my trying to "keep it together" I missed a truth: There's strength in weakness! 2 Corinthians 12:10 reminds us when we're weak, we're strong in CHRIST! So why do we attempt to hold it together with our human strength? Jesus said in Matthew 11:28 "Come to me all who are weary and heavy burdened and I will give you rest" On this day whatever has you weak, release it to God. How do you withstand the turmoil, heartache or pain of your situation? Remember God gives sufficient grace for the storms. We spend our whole lives trying to avoid hard times instead of finding God faithful and sufficient in the midst of whatever situation He allows. Our weakness opens the flow of God's strength. Only when you're personally weak can you experience this supernatural strength. Let this day be a day where God releases the strength you need. The strength of His word that sustains us and according to Isaiah 55:11 is not permitted to return to Him void. His Word must prosper and accomplish what He sent it to do! PERFORM!

Scripture: {Isaiah 40:29-31 Nkjv} He gives power to the weak, And to those who have no might He increases strength. Even the youths shall faint and be weary, And the young men shall utterly fall, But those who wait on the Lord Shall renew their strength; They shall mount up with wings like eagles, They shall run and not be weary, They shall walk and not faint.

***Prayer:** Lord, help me in everything I'm weary in. My energy and motivation is (s)lacking. I need your strength to get back in alignment with your will for my life. I need your joy to be my strength! I need your peace to consume me! The pressure (be specific) in this season has pushed me into a corner and I need your reinforcement to help me move forward. My* *desire is to run the race faithfully, finding refuge in the secret place of Psalm 91 (read Psalm 91; make it a part of your prayer). Strengthen my mind to avoid temptation that keep me stagnated, doubting and lazy! Strengthen my heart and mind that I'm able to say yes (again) to the life you ordered for me. You are my rock! I believe you will lift up my heavy arms and I will be restored for the tasks you put before me! I believe your joy will completely consume the weakness of my life and make me strong again. I will not be grounded or limited. I will mount up with wings like an eagle and soar beyond my today! With your supernatural power I will overcome all obstacles in my path because in my weakness your power will be made known!*

DAY 5

"NO REQUEST - GRATEFUL FOR GRACE"

...Loving on God while listening! Worship!

When you've done the usual; praising, examining your life, sharing it all with the Lord and you still feel like you're in the room alone, try letting Him talk to you! Often times we don't take time to worship God. Of course our lives should worship Him but I learned some of my greatest battles were won when I set time apart to worship Him. Acknowledging who He is to me: A healer (spiritually and naturally), a provider, my strength and a mind regulator always helps me stand in confidence. There are times when prayer should consist of just worship. No need to ask for a thing, just thank Him for who He is and what He's already done. When you openly acknowledge who He is and express it in prayer time, if gives you peace in the midst of anything. God saw that we are in need of salvation yet unworthy of it. {John 3:16 Nkjv} "God so loved the world that He gave His only begotten Son that whoever believes in him should not perish but have everlasting life". Salvation is a wonderful thing! It gives us access to eternity with Christ. We must always remain humbled and grateful for the grace of God. Today, express your gratitude in prayer towards God for Him simply being who He is. Almighty and All Powerful! As you take this time to pray, visualize moments when life should have been another way for you but because He loved you beyond your issues and faults, He keep you as His own. As His own, His eyes are always on you and His ears are always attentive to you (1 Peter 3:12) He allows His Word to be a lamp unto your feet, a light to your path (Psalm 119:105). He is your help (Hebrew 13:5-6). You've been redeemed and He promises to be with you through all things, no matter the circumstance or situation (Isaiah 43:1-3). Be thankful for any undeserved grace given by anyone but be forever grateful for the gift of grace God gave through the sacrifice of Jesus Christ that entitled us to salvation. Worship must be vital and real from within and it must be based on a true perception of God! Worship must engage your emotions and worship must engage your thoughts. Our worship shows our adoration and loyalty to God for His grace. Love up on God and allow Him to minister to you

Scripture: {Titus 2:11 Nkjv} For the grace of God that brings salvation has appeared to all men

***Prayer**: Heavenly Father, I don't ask for anything but humbly give thanks for all You have done! I appreciate you for sending Your Son to die on the cross to redeem me of our sins. Thank you for enduring the pain and suffering for our salvation. (Openly express all the things great and small that God has done for you, your family, your friends, your country, etc.) As you continue on this journey of the Personal Prayer Revival, continue to allow this to be you're opening communication with God!)*

DAY 6

"INTERCESSION"

...Declaring, decreeing, in the gap fighting for others! There must always be a time where we pray for one another.

On this day you take the place of others and pray on their behalf. You can even write a list of people you want to or feel led to pray for. If you have specifics than it's important to pray for them according to God's Word. If you don't have specifics to pray for, then you must allow the Holy Spirit to lead you in what to pray for. As the Holy Spirit shows you the identity of specific strongholds on others lives, take authority over the stronghold though Jesus Christ. God's Spirit is in you and more powerful than that which that is in this world (1 John 4:4) What may be revealed to you during this time of intercession for someone else should never be revealed to anyone else. (Unless God leads you otherwise). Your "intercession" should always be scripture led. With it being scripture led, you're bringing the person/situation/circumstance under subjection to God's Word. With intercession you must be consistent and committed with the tenacity to not give in or give up through prayer which can sometimes land us in warfare. You are now standing in the gap for others! If you want to break down a wall, a good strategy would be to have you chip away at any gaps in the wall. If you chip away at the gaps, the wall will eventually lack the support needed to stand and give way. The book of Nehemiah will give you a great example of standing in the gap. Nehemiah was given permission to go back to help rebuild Jerusalem. Upon Nehemiah's arrival he witnessed the city lying in ruins and the people in despair. He gathered the people to help rebuild the city's wall. Well when they started rebuilding, other countries began to make trouble for them hoping they'd stop building. Nehemiah instructed those that were soldiers (who were also building) to keep building in one hand but to hold their sword in the other hand to fight. Uncovered gaps in the wall would make Jerusalem incomplete and vulnerable. So soldiers stood in the gap ready to fight! We will always have weak spots in our lives. The adversary will always attempt to hinder us from building our lives in Christ. But God will use people like you to stand in the gap and fight through prayer for others. God's not looking for perfect prayer warriors. He's looking for those who have faith and a willing heart, who want to see His will manifested in the lives of others. Intercession involves taking hold of God's will and refusing to let go until His will is manifested! Today you will grab hold of others purpose and destiny and fight for it. Today's time of prayer is key to seeing breakthroughs in the lives of others. Pray for the hearts and minds of people! Pray for circumstances that people are dealing with that hinder their success. Bind the work of Satan! Jesus has given you authority to defeat the power of the enemy (Luke 10:19). Don't be distracted during this time of intercession. Don't allow your mind to wander from your purpose in prayer. STAY FOCUSED! Through intercession, you take the offensive side in the battle, building up your family, friends, associates, community, nations and even the world! Just as you are interceding for someone else, Jesus is making intercession for us all! (Hebrews 7:25) He has also put you on the heart and mind of others!

Scripture: {2 Corinthians 1:8-11 Msg} We don't want you in the dark, friends, about how hard it was when all this came down on us in Asia province. It was so bad we didn't think we were going to make it. We felt like we'd been sent to death row, that it was all over for us. As it turned out, it was the best thing that could have happened. Instead of trusting in our own strength or wits to get out of it, we were forced to trust God totally—not a bad idea since he's the God who raises the dead! And he did it, rescued us from certain doom. *And* he'll do it again, rescuing us as many times as we need rescuing. YOU and YOUR PRAYERS are part of the rescue operation. I don't want you in the dark about that either. I can see your faces even now, lifted in praise for God's deliverance of us, a rescue in which your prayers played such a crucial part.

__Prayer:__ Lord! I come into Your presence and ask You to give me the heart of the intercessor. Open my eyes and ears that I may meet the needs of your people through prayer. Help me to be persistent in prayer until the breakthrough comes. (Begin to pray for the list you've created and those the Holy Spirit lead you to pray for. This prayer also trains you up to hear and act on the leading of the Holy Spirit.)

DAY 7

"RENEW MY MIND"

Lord, reveal Your will (again) Take me back to the heart of worship! Show me how to work the Word in a way that is pleasing unto You and tangible unto others!

It is so easy to become common with God! Especially when you're use to a routine, Sunday church at 10:00am. Bible Study on Wednesday at 7:30pm. Prayer on Friday at 8:00pm. Fast when the Pastor calls for a fast and prayer when you're going through. We have to be very careful not to become complacent in living for God. Our mind ought to be renewed daily! I've learned to look and listen for God in all things, expecting to see and hear Him in newness daily; which does not allow me to put Him in a box. Out of formalities and tradition we often lose our steps ordered by God which takes us out of His will. I remember when I was first called to Pastor. God showed me how my church would be slightly different than the traditional church. I was excited in the beginning because my passion was for the "unchurched;" those that didn't know how to do traditional church. Until many from the "traditional" church that I looked up to shunned me away for doing things differently. I would oftentimes try to conform to ways that weren't necessarily wrong but weren't what God called me to do. I stepped out of the will of God for my life to appease others. The joy I once had, I had no more. The heart of worship; a life that was pleasing to God which brought me strength and peace I had no more. I became complacent and accepted this way of life while hindering the will of God for me. With complacency we wander from the heart of God and our expectation of Him is dimmed. We lose passion for His Word. With passion for God's Word we pursue to live according to it and if we're living according it, we have what is says we can have and we can be who it says we are! When we first said yes to Him or even after we said yes to His plans, we believed all things to be possible. Otherwise we wouldn't have said yes. When we started out we believed His will was for us to be saved and free. We believed He had great things for our lives so we were willing to do whatever was possible with the expectation of Him doing what we believed He could do for us. Sometimes "process" wears our mind down. When having to go through a process, it sometimes makes us lose focus of God's will for our lives, especially when process is uncomfortable and unfamiliar. I had to learn how to embrace process while keeping my mind stayed on Him. With a renewed mind, you seek out God's standard and not your own. A renewed mind will bring about new behavior. During this dedicated time of praying to God for 30 days I had to ask God to reveal His will again where it was all about HIM and His desire for my life. I needed Him to revive the visions, dreams and assignments that I may get back to the heart of worship with my life. A renewed mind is a process. Not a one time achievement. You must train your mind to be in alignment with Philippians 4:8, "Finally, brethren, whatsoever things are true, whatsoever things are honest, whatsoever things are just, whatsoever things are pure, whatsoever things are lovely, whatsoever things are of good report; if there be any virtue, and if there be any praise, THINK on these things." The importance of your mind being renewed is not only for you to get back on track and stay on track, but it's also purposed for those watching you, gleaning from you that they too would see, the perfect place is in the will of God! In His will you witness, "ALL things are possible!"

Scripture: {Ephesians 4:20-24 Nlv} But you did not learn anything like this from Christ. If you have heard of Him and have learned from Him, put away the old person you used to be. Have nothing to do with your old sinful life. It was sinful because of being fooled into following bad desires. Let your minds and hearts be made new. You must become a new person and be God-like. Then you will be made right with God and have a true holy life.

Prayer: Dear Lord! My desire is to live a life that is pleasing to you! Today I pray for the renewal of my mind. Today I submit myself to Your Word which is able to expose and discern the very thoughts and purposes of my heart. The weapons of my warfare are not carnal, but mighty through You to the pulling down of strongholds of my mind. I come against all things that exalt itself against the true knowledge of who You are and I lead every thought captive to the obedience of You! Today I pray for transformation through the renewing of my mind. Fill my thoughts with images of your reality, your truth! Empower me to gird up the loins of my mind, to aim my mind toward heavenly things, to reckon on my new mindset, and to rest in my mindset in Christ."

DAY 8

"ASK, SEEK, KNOCK"

Pour out your hearts desires to God. Declare, decree and believe in the release of some specific promises!

Learn to ask God for whatever you desire! When we pray we ought to pray in harmony with the view of God we have. Sometimes our view of God can be influenced by our earthly view of humans. The individual who believes that God is one who is full of wrath, fickle or not trustworthy will be less likely to ask Him for anything. But the individual who believes that God is gracious, trustworthy and faithful will come boldly. In Matthew 9, two blind men were following Jesus crying out, "Have mercy on us." Jesus asked the blind men, "Do you believe that I am able to heal you?" They said, "Yes, we believe." Jesus touched their eyes and said, "You believe (according to your faith) I can heal your eyes, so it will happen." Don't be afraid to ask God for what you deem as a hard thing! We don't always get what we ask for. For example: wrong motives will hinder answers to prayer. The more time we spend communing with God, the more we will know what to ask for in accordance to His will. Prayer shows dependence of God for needs that can be met no other way. God is always pleased with such displays of faith. In Matthew 7:7 Jesus was telling His disciples to pray but He was also giving them instructions on how to see their prayers answered.

ASK: Although God knows what we need before we ask Him, He usually won't provide some things until we ask. It is not that He is unaware of our needs. According to (Matthew 6:8) He knows what we need before we ask. Asking (and receiving) not only draws us to communicate with God but it also builds our faith and relationship with Him. God wants us to communicate with Him and sometimes He draws us to prayer through our needs.

SEEK: It's not always enough just to ask. More often than not, you also have to seek. If you're asking God for a new house, seek it in faith. If you're asking Him for restoration, seek restoration. If you're asking Him for healing, seek healing. Ask what you desire and seek it in faith. (James 2:26) Faith without works is dead. If you desire a millionaire status, you can't always just sit back and wait for God to drop it out of the sky. Seek out ways to save, be a good steward and invest. Put your desires and needs before Him through asking and then seek out the strategies of God to receive.

KNOCK: If you seek, you will find. Once you see God's promise in clear view, knock until the door is opened. Be in pursuit of it! Take action!

Today we will ask in faith and act in faith!

Scripture: {Matthew 7:7-8 Kjv} Ask, and it shall be given to you; seek, and ye shall find; knock, and it shall be opened unto you: For every one that asketh receiveth; and he that seeketh findeth; and to him that knocketh it shall be opened.

Prayer: *Dear Heavenly Father, I know that you said whatever I ask for, through faith I shall receive. If I seek, I will surely find. And if I knock, doors will open that no man can shut. I request opportunities, abundant blessings & favor. Lord, I seek direction to every open door you have for me. Open up the eyes of my faith. Help me not only to see doors but to boldly knock and enter in. I have Faith in You... You alone are God, the only One God and all things are possible by You.*

DAY 9

"RESTORATION"

Lord help those you sent to lead! Strengthen the hearts and minds of those who continue to run on in You and deliver the hearts and minds of those who grew weary & fainted, stole your glory and/or rejected You!

On this day we pray for leaders. Those whom God called to lead but have become weary or have been deceived and submitted to sin. Know that our continued growth in God is effective with the help of those He called to lead us. I remember the election 2016 when President Trump was elected. A lot of churches were devastated and angry. Many were concerned because of Trump's morals. They believed we would suffer at the hands of Trump. The Lord challenged me to begin praying for Leaders of the Body of Christ. Leaders are given a great responsibility to guide, instruct and lead, especially in a time like that. If we have leaders with clean hands and pure hearts, then those who have a desire to fulfill God's purpose for their lives have the reinforcement they need. Leaders cannot do this alone. They need people that will commit to praying for them. Leaders are human. They face the same challenges as everyone else, if not more or greater. They grow tired in ministry and are tempted by sin just as others do. As leader, they become the "face" of Christ and we know the enemy in the world wants to paint a false picture of who Christ really is. James 3:1 says, "Not many of you should become teachers, my fellow believers, because you know that we who teach will be judged more strictly." Leaders carry a degree of responsibility to their followers. They are often the targets. We must pray for them recognizing the greatness of their task and because we are grateful for their willingness to lead. Praying for leaders *(your Pastor specifically if you have one)* is imperative to their spiritual health. Though you will pray however the Holy Spirit leads you, it is even ok to ask leaders if there is anything specific they need prayer for. Pray for that. Remember prayer is an intimate time with God and all things during that intimate time should be kept between you and God. (Unless He instructs otherwise). It's important to pray that leaders will keep God's heart in the forefront of all things. Pray that they will cultivate strong character and uncompromising integrity. As you stood in the gap for others on Day 6, today you will stand in the gap specifically for leaders. They need your prayers and you need their purpose. As a leader, they're not exempt from falling. Truth be told, it seems as if they fall harder but we are to uplift those that have even fell. While praying for those who are still in the perfect will of God, we must still pray for those who've stepped out of His will. Galatians 6:1 instructs us, "Brethren, even if a man is caught in any trespass, you who are spiritual, restore such a one in a spirit of gentleness" The ministry of restoring a fallen Leader belongs to all who are spiritual. While it's never easy, it is vital to the health of the Body of Christ. Remember we're all humans, we all fall short of God's glory but when we cover each other in prayer especially those who have a charge to lead we become helpers of one another. We must constantly intercede for those who lead that they don't fall at the hands of the adversary as well as pray for those who have fallen from Grace.

Scripture: {Jeremiah 29:7 Niv} Also, seek the peace and prosperity of the city to which I have carried you into exile. Pray to the LORD for it, because if it prospers, you too will prosper."

Prayer: *Father, in the name of Jesus, I pray that, the spirit of wisdom and understanding and knowledge shall rest upon our Pastors and all leaders of the church. Keep them from losing heart when ministry gets tough. Help them prove faithful with the things you have entrusted to him. Teach them Your ways so that they know You and find favor with You as they lead us. Keep them open and honest before You and help them to represent the truth. I pray that they would love and serve their families with glad hearts and that their family would support what You called them to do. I pray for a passion; for conviction and dedication to their calling. I pray that they will walk in confidence while kneeling in humility. I pray for encouragement in their faith and ministry, and against those who attack, slander, harm, or speak evil against them. I pray that you cover them from depression. I pray that they will never fall prey to envy, jealousy, insecurity, or comparison. I pray for their holiness and purity, and against lust, affairs, love of money, and pride. I pray for rest spiritually and physically. Continue to give them revelation, clarity and peace. Restore those who have fallen. Let Your Word speak to them in their darkest place. Open their eyes and ears that they see and hear your conviction. Remove people and things* *that have caused them to go astray. Let their minds remember their assignments and who You are to them.*

DAY 10

ENCOURAGE YOURSELF

Release everything today! Though you've been praying for the last 9 days, I'm sure there is something you haven't touched on. You've been focused and making efforts to be on point. RESTORATION HAS STARTED! The adversary wants you to believe it's all in vain. He wants you to quit! Quitting is an option that you must refuse to choose. Today I want you to pray however you feel or are led. FREE your mind today of anything that has been trying to linger on and hinder you. Whether it be the children, your spouse, coworker, your house, your job, just give it to God today! Grab some "encouraging" scripture and say them out loud! If all is well, then today you ought to simply make this whole prayer about God. Tell Him how thankful you are about some specific things that you have obtained in these first 9 days!

Scripture: {Isaiah 40:31 Niv} but those who hope in the LORD will renew their strength. They will soar on wings like eagles; they will run and not grow weary, they will walk and not be faint.

Prayer: *Dear Heavenly Father… (you finish the rest! LET GO & LET GOD!)*

DAY 11

"PROTECTION"

Important people are protected by bodyguards! People like the POTUS & FLOTUS, celebrities, the Pope, Ambassadors, Queen of England and of course the children of God. We are a part of a dangerous world; naturally & spiritually. Important people are some of the most attacked! Though we should be praying daily for the protection from all hurt, harm and danger, today we will pray for supernatural protection. One of the greatest shields of protection is PEACE! Have you ever been in a chaotic situation and because of the peace of God, the situation didn't seem so chaotic after all? The situation may have been conflicting but the peace of God shaped your perspective. The peace of God that surpasses all understanding and PROTECTS your heart and mind. God designed for you to live a life of victory over the tyranny of your circumstances and problems you face. Unfortunately, we don't always experience this peace God wants us to have. God desires to have us in a place where we can be at peace and rest our minds. David wrote in Psalms 3:5-6 (Msg) "I stretch myself out. I sleep, then I'm up again, rested, tall and steady, fearless before the enemy mobs coming from all sides." Even though he was surrounded by enemies and he was facing many difficulties, trials and tribulations, he was able to rest. He was protected by the peace of God. The assurance, the Lord was with him and looking after him. The peace that God provides is not dependent upon the quieting of our circumstance nor does it mean the absence of conflict. The peace that God provides is dependent upon your trust and faith in Him. Today, pray for the peace that consumes your heart! It protects your heart and mind regardless of the tempest raging. This peace is important to live a Godly life! It's important to us as individuals because we need to experience God's peace personally to face our own circumstances and it's important if we're going to be witnesses for Christ. The world is always watching and looking for answers. They're not always interested in listening to what you say but they pay attention to what you do! If you go through tragedy or difficulties and they realize that you are able to triumph, it draws them to this God who offers a sustaining peace. The world's peace depends on having favorable circumstances. If things are going well, then they feel peaceful. When things go awry, the peace quickly fades. Jesus made the distinction between His peace and the world's peace in John 14:27. He said, "Peace I leave with you; my peace I give you. I do not give to you as the world gives." The one who places their full confidence in God in every circumstance will possess supernatural peace. An inner calm will consume the heart. Because we're humans, we will have "heart" encounters with fear, doubt, worry, etc. It is God's peace that protects us from those things. Your heart is the subfloor of your emotion. It's the part that acts or reacts to life issues and circumstances. What your heart is made up of causes anxiety or worry (emotions) and your mind puts the things of the heart in motion. Your heart and mind is who your are and it needs to be protected by God's peace!

Scripture: {Philippians 4:7 Nkjv} And the peace of God, which passeth all understanding, shall keep your hearts and minds through Christ Jesus.

Prayer*: Lord, manifest Philippians 4:7. My desire is to live an unstoppable life through you! I desire to excel, succeed, accomplish and fulfill all you've destined me for. In Your Word you said, in this world there will trouble. Because I am in this world but not of this world, I pray for your protections of peace. Still my heart and quiet my soul that I may learn to trust and wait upon you. (Admit things that you've been worrying about. Give them to God and pray His peace will overtake those areas of worry/doubt) Help me to put my trust in day by day. Protect my mind from doubt, worry and anxiety.*

DAY 12

"DECLARING"

Healing; Physically or Spiritually

By Day 12 you should have already witnessed some personal miracles. Whether it has been in your life or the lives of those you prayed for. Let what you've seen manifested, accelerate your faith. Declare what you desire and what you believe! Be proactive and decisive as you declare God's Word. God has given the promise that whatsoever you declare in Jesus name it will be done! (John 14:13-14 Kjv) "And whatsoever ye shall ask in my name, that will I do, that the Father may be glorified in the Son. If ye shall ask any thing in my name, I will do it." God delegated authority to you, as a believer, that you may accomplish His will. You are responsible to speak in accordance with God's will that has been spoken concerning you! When the weather is bad and the roads are deemed unsafe, the government usually declares a state of emergency! The government makes it KNOWN what is happening and those who hear it must adhere to it. Countries make a "declaration of war" which means that they make known that a state of war now exist and we must adhere and prepare. As you declare God's Word of healing over your life (or others) what and whoever hears it, must adhere to the declaration. According to Proverbs 18:21 and Proverbs 15:4, your tongue is a powerful tool! (Proverbs 18:2) "Life and death are in the power of the tongue." (Proverbs 15:4) "A wholesome tongue is a tree of life: but perverseness therein is a breach in the spirit." You have the authority to speak God's Word and what you speak has power! Throughout the Word of God, God called His people to take command of their destiny's; order with authority, take charge of it, exercise direct authority over it and dominate by position. Declaring can be and is essential in prayer because we are to speak God's Word but declaration is not the prayer. You must use your authority and power to declare a thing while in prayer. Proclaim the truth of what God has revealed in His Word. Declaring does not make something truth, it acknowledges and makes known what is already true; His Word concerning our lives. Speak the answers. NOT the problems! Declaration provokes change in the situation or one who hears it. We can make declarations in order to make known these truths. This can be spoken to God as a part of prayer or about God as a weapon in prayer. We can establish and align our spiritual atmosphere by making declarations concerning the truth of who God is, what Christ has done, who Christ now is, and what He will do, as well as who we are in Christ. We can also declare to demonic spirits the truth about who we are in Christ, our victory and dominion (through Christ) over Satan and His kingdom. In making declarations, we do not create something new or bring into exist a new reality but we align ourselves with the truth of God as it is revealed in His word.

Declaring has no value without faith in the Word! Words that are in agreement with God's Word propel us to the place of manifestation. Declaring God's word over your life should be a daily thing. Be in agreement with what the Word says about you (and others) and speak it! With what was read about "declaring", if you or anyone you know needs healing, whether it be mentally, spiritually or physically today take your declarations in prayer! Pray God's Word!

Scripture: {Psalm 73:28 Kjv} But it is good for me to draw near to God; I have put my trust in the Lord God, that I may declare all thy works.

Prayer: *Jehovah Rapha (my healer) I declare every stronghold over my life is broken. Through faith in you I have been declared righteous before You. Your Word {Romans 8:11} says if Your spirit dwells in me, you will give life to my mortal body through the Spirit of Jesus. I claim this Word as mine right now and take hold of it by faith! Your Word {1 Corinthians 6:15} declares that my body is a member of Christ. As a member of Christ surely sickness and disease are not mine. I reject all forms of sickness and declare total healing. According to God's Word {Mark 9:23} all things are possible to those who believe. I declare by faith that my body, mind & heart is healed. With my heart and my mouth, I speak life and healing over myself. (Remember, you are taking your declaration INTO prayer so as you humbly speak to God, confidently speak to Satan with your power and authority) Satan, I declare to you in Jesus name you have not right or authority over me. According to God's Word {Matthew 18:18} Whatever I bind on earth is bound in heaven. I bind you from operating against me anyway. Every curse of infirmity, sickness or premature death, witchcraft and destruction is broken off of my life. I take my stand as one who is redeemed from any curse you bring upon me. I* *command it to leave and return no more. According to {Isaiah 53} by Jesus stripes I am healed. He took my sickness and carried my pain. It is the will of God that I be healed. (You can also begin to call out sickness that you have or are in your bloodline. As you are praying for physical healing remember to pray for any areas of spiritual healing as well) **Personalize the Word of God by speaking in "I" "Me" "My" terms or if you're declaring the Word for someone else use their name. Example: {Isaiah 53:5 Nkjv} But He was wounded for our (MY) transgressions and He was bruised for our (MY) iniquities; the chastisement of our (MY) peace was upon Him and by His stripes we were (I AM) healed. **Write declarations down, memorize them and make them a part of your life daily (language).*

DAY 13

"COVERED"

No weapon formed against you shall prosper! As you continue to grow during this journey it's important to cover yourself with truth. Of course the adversary is angry with you and will pull out all stops to hinder you from reaching your 30 Day mark. The manifesting of "REVIVAL" has begun to hit your life and though you're at a place where you're feeling better, maybe even unstoppable, satan will not stop. When the children of Israel were headed to the land God promised, the enemy of their minds constantly tried to hinder them from going forth. He made them feel like their journey was pointless because it wasn't a quick thing. It wasn't always glamorous and they didn't quite understand the journey they were on. Before the children of Israel were brought out of bondage, God already revealed to Moses in Exodus 6:6-8 that He was going to free them, take them as His own, become their loving God and give them possession of the Promised Land. According to Exodus 3:8, the Promised Land was a land flowing with milk and honey. I'm sure when they first heard the great news of freedom they were excited but probably didn't realize their journey would take them through the "wilderness;" The same place Satan met up with Jesus (Matthew 4) and tried to hinder Him from fulfilling what He was sent to the earth to do. It is the adversary's plan to hinder you from completing a task, especially when the task lands you in or keeps you in the will of God. Many of you picked up this book and thought, "ahhh, a Personal Revival, just what I need!" and was excited about the course! But you found yourself at times wondering, "is this pointless. Is this in vain?" The truth is, this journey for you is well worth it! According to 1 Corinthians 15:58, if you're steadfast and immovable, abounding in the work of the Lord, than your labor IS NOT in vain! You're simply under attack! Like the children of Israel before they experienced the promise, God already prepared it for them. God purposed this 30 Day journey for you and the adversary will do anything to stop you. This 30 Day journey can set you up for the rest of your life. The truth is God set you up for this and it's important to keep your mind covered in truth! I'm sure you've noticed already, 12 days in all type of weapons have formed against you to provoke you to quit. Be excited because you made it this far. You can't afford to entertain weapons that have formed to stop you. The truth is, "They won't prosper!" They don't have what it takes to stop you, especially when you are fully covered in the full armor of God! (Ephesians 6:13-18) Let your prayers go forth that you are covered from the seen and the unseen. With a covered mind you combat the adversary, dismantling His successful manifestation in your life.

Scripture: {Ephesians 6:13 Nkjv} Wherefore take unto you the whole armor of God, that ye may be able to withstand in the evil day, and having done all, to stand.

Prayer*: Lord, I follow your command to put on the full armor of God because my battle is not against flesh and blood but against rulers, authorities, the powers of* *this dark world and against spiritual forces of evil in the unseen world. May I be covered by your truth; the belt of truth that holds me up by the truth of your Word. (What is His truth for your life? DECLARE IT). May I be covered with the gospel shoes of peace that I may stand on your good news! A firm foundation; Jesus Christ. That my foot shall not slip but be firm on you! May I be covered with the helmet of Salvation that my mind is protected from thoughts that would distract me or lead me out of your will. That my mind won't be double minded but stayed on the blood of Christ that set me free. May I be covered with the breastplate of righteousness that I would walk in integrity and a good character. That my heart and mind will be protected from deceit and ill motives and that every vulnerable place in my life with be strengthened. May I be covered with shield of faith, that I would not be moved by every weapon that's formed against me to slow me down, hinder me or stop me spiritually, emotionally, mentally or physically. That I would have the courage to faith forward in all that you've destined for my life. Cover me with the sword of the spirit, Your Word, that I would prepare with it for all encounters in my life. That it would give insight, guidance, counsel, wisdom and strategies. Cover me from the seen & unseen!*

DAY 14

"CASTING DOWN"

Deliver me from mental strongholds!

You are great! You are favored! You are qualified! {Romans 8:29-30 Nkjv} "Moreover whom He predestined, these He also called; whom He called, these He also justified; and whom He justified, these He also glorified." You have power. NOW WALK, TALK and LIVE IN AUTHORITY. It's important to know WHO you are in God! When you come into the knowledge of who you are, you destroy everything about you that is not of God! Mental rejection, persecution, affliction, lack, and disqualification are all things used against you to stop you from progressing. The devil uses strongholds to bring complication, hindrance and to destroy our faith in God. Strongholds are built upon deception. These deceptions which form strongholds can come from a wide variety of sources, including our environment, those around us, our parents or even demonic spirits. Many people are living a defeated life because of what we choose to believe. If you believe you are insignificant, then you'll live your life believing you're not important. For us to live in victory it is very important for us to have the right thinking. Our thoughts are very powerful as they govern our behavior and our behavior governs our lives. Strongholds are targeted at our minds and our real problems are not the trials and temptations we go through, but what we believe and where we put our faith and trust in the midst of the problems. What you allow to capture your mind and heart is what will determine your outcome in situations. Casting down strongholds from the enemy is a great tool of spiritual warfare, and one of the first strategies that you must use to experience victories. You must cast down and not exalt images that try to be above the Word of God and what is says about you. Example: when the devil says that you are going to die, you cannot exalt what the devil says, rather declare and exalt the Word of God, which says, {Psalms 118:17 Kjv}"I shall not die, but live, and declare the works of the Lord." Don't exalt the devil's lies for your life by believing it and putting it above the Word of God. Rather cast it down and bring it under subjection or captivity by making it (the devil's words) obedient to Christ. As long as Satan can hold you in the arena of lies, he'll defeat you. But if you hold Satan in the arena of faith, you'll defeat him in every battle. When the devil tries to bring a thought or image into your mind, refuse to receive it. Begin to declare the Word of God regarding how God views you or the situation that the enemy is trying to get you to think on. *Too much carnal and worldly things make you weak in the spirit and unable to discipline yourself to become a person of faith and power*. To actively cast down imaginations of the enemy, you must remain a person of prayer and a hearer and doer of God's Word. This kind of person will be alert to spiritual things. You can't cast down strongholds, if you don't have God's thoughts or vision for you. You must strengthen yourself spiritually by allowing the Word of God to become your foundation. (Casting down may also consist of fasting & consecrating). As you pray this day, recognize the negativity that's supposed to leave a negative impact on your life and see how even the negative can work for your good! Cast down the thoughts of failure because of those things listed below and recognize God's ability to perfect you by the circumstances. {Romans 8:28} "And we know that all things work together for good to those who love God, to those who are the called according to His purpose."

Rejection defines God's will that you stand out and be the influence the world needs.

Persecution equips you to stand in the end times and sets you up to reign.

Affliction presents opportunity for God to expose His power through you!

Lack challenges you to discover the power that works in you.

Being disqualified or **_Counted out_** keeps you humble before the Father that He may position you before "the people" as proof and hope of His delivering power. (For some He wants to show He does as He pleases with whom He chooses).

Scripture: {2 Corinthians 10:4-5 Nkjv} "For the weapons of our warfare are not carnal, but mighty through God to the pulling down of strongholds; Casting down imaginations, and every high thing that exalted itself against the knowledge of God, and bringing into captivity every thought to the obedience of Christ;

Prayer: *I cast down imaginations and reasoning's. I bring every thought captive to the obedience of Jesus Christ. If the thought doesn't line up with the Word of God, I reject it. I believe and think on only what God's Word says. I pray that You would break any stronghold of fear, doubt, shame or unbelief (name every and any stronghold you recognize in your life) that weakens my walk and witness and makes me vulnerable to the lies of the devil. Teach me how to resist the devil and to take every thought that attempts to take my life captive. You have not given me the spirit of fear, but of power, love, self-discipline and a sound mind! Reveal to me any habits that have become strongholds. Give me the grace to admit my faults and turn from everything that keeps me a slave to the devil. Expose the strategies of the enemy and give me vision and understanding to know what, when and how to pray your will.*

DAY 15

"VALUE VISION"

Protect my heart from those who openly love while secretly despising who You created me to be and what you created me to do. Reveal my heart to those that have a desire to see Your will manifested through me and to those who have the ability to support it coming to pass.

Your vision for your life is one of the most important things in your walk with Christ. {Proverbs 29:18} This scripture teaches us without vision, we perish. You need to always see beyond where you are. When your vision is on what's above, greater or what's to come, you're more driven to pursue it. You want to connect with people who truly value your vision. When someone values your vision, they value you! Your purpose is important to them and they support your purpose being fulfilled. When you're connected to people that openly push you but secretly despise (jealous/envy) you, they'll never help you maximize your potential. If you're expecting to go beyond where you are now, you need people that expect you to go beyond as well. You need people that are willing to help as if it were their own vision. Often times this isn't your close friend or even family; those who are familiar with you. You have to be ok with having friends and family for fun and friends and family for ministry. There's a difference. When vision is involved you can't afford to be careless. You need God to send you those that not only receive from you but are able to also pour into you, seeking nothing in return. You need people that see the bigger picture of your purpose and how fulfilling your purpose will affect the Kingdom. These people desire to see you win even if it means it's not their turn yet.

VALUE: the importance, worth, or usefulness of something.

VISION: the act or power of anticipating that which will or may come to be.

Scripture: {Philippians 2:4 Erv} Don't be interested only in your own life, but care about the lives of others too.

Prayer: *Father, I may be blind to those who mean me no good. Help me see the truth. Apply the power of Your Word to my heart and mind. Connect me with people that value me and my vision. Send me people that refresh my life, hold me accountable, build me up, strengthen me, challenge me, walk in integrity, wisdom and love. Send me people with like minds, that keep you first in all things. Give me wisdom with my relationship. My desire is to excel in you, send me people that have the same desire. Help me Lord not to push those you send away. Heal me of all hurt from past friendship that I don't push away those that you send. Expose their hearts to me Lord and give me the boldness to end all toxic relationships.*

DAY 16

"TRANSFORM"

Create in me a clean heart. Empty it of those things that I selfishly hold there and fill it up with more of you, your character, your desires, your ways.

Transformation is a process. Like the caterpillar that enters a cocoon and after time transform into a butterfly, we too must go through a transformation process. Getting saved was the first process of our transformation. When we got saved God didn't take away our free will. We must still seek out His ways to become better and more like Him. Though our desire is to be Christ like, I'm sure you've recognized it's not an easy task. Paul said, {Romans 12:2} "And be not conformed to this world: but be ye <u>transformed by the renewing of your mind</u>..." What we do and how we think affects how we feel. How we feel influences our desires and our desires produce our actions. If our mind is consumed with ways and things that are contrary to God's purpose for our lives, then our actions take us out of His will. Satan uses different things to influence your thoughts; a strategy to keep you stuck. For example, when we are self-righteous our thoughts have us seeking a satisfaction of impressing God (or people) with our goodness. When we gossip, our thoughts have us seeking a satisfaction of feeling better than others or even sowing discord. When we're bitter, our thoughts have us seeking a satisfaction of being a victim. These are all sinful and some tactics used to keep us stuck in our growth in

God. God has a plan for your life. With every passing day, experience, opportunity, trial, victory, lesson, and more, you are being transformed into the likeness of Christ. God does the hard work. He is the "Potter," we are the clay. It is up to us to be willing, disciplined participants in the process in order to reap the reward of transformation. Transformation is critical. It reflects the likeness and glory of Christ. Today our desire & prayer is for our minds to be transformed into the likeness of Christ. Jesus promised us in Luke 11:13 that we would experience more of the Spirit's work by praying earnestly for it! Through this prayer expect to experience the Holy Spirit enabling you to see and feel Christ glory! As our hearts are filled with more of Christ, we will be set free from desires that are not of His character.

Scripture: {Ephesians 4:20-23 Kjv} But you have not so learned Christ, if indeed you have heard Him and have been taught by Him, as the truth is in Jesus: that you put off, concerning your former conduct, the old man which grows corrupt according to the deceitful lusts, and be renewed in the spirit of your mind, and that you put on the new man which was created according to God, in true righteousness and holiness.

Prayer: Dear Lord, help me to understand your Word & your will that I may grow in the knowledge of who you are. Enable me to obey your commands that your will may be fulfilled in my life. Transform me into your likeness through the Holy Spirit. I'm making myself 100% available to be transformed by you. I desire to be transformed by you and allow your life to be expressed through me. Allow me to discern between flesh and spirit so that I can choose to walk by your spirit. Give me spiritual awareness that I don't conform to the ways of the world. Open the eyes of our heart to see how you are revealing your truths to us in our everyday life. I desire to turn from my old way of thinking and turn towards you. Take out what needs to be taken out (Feel free to list or be specific about anything you notice in you that is worldly) and fill every empty place within with your spirit.

DAY 17

"BREATHE"

Help me to take on today's challenges! Expose the opportunities hidden in them. Show me the miracle that is being created through them.

Genesis 2:7 says "Then the Lord God formed the man of dust from the ground and _breathed into his nostrils the breath of life, and the man became a living creature_." Ezekiel 37:7-10 says "I prophesied just as I'd been commanded. As I prophesied, there was a sound and, oh, rustling! The bones moved and came together, bone to bone. I kept watching. Sinews formed, then muscles on the bones, then skin stretched over them. But they had no breath in them. He said to me, "Prophesy to the breath. Prophesy, son of man. Tell the breath, 'God, the Master, says, Come from the four winds. Come, breath. Breath on these slain bodies. Breath life! So I prophesied, just as he commanded me. _The breathe entered them and they came alive_! They stood up on their feet, a huge army." When God created Adam he was just dust. It wasn't until He breathed into his nostrils did Adam become the miracle! He became a living creature! When God instructed Ezekiel to prophesy to the dry bones, they didn't became effective (a strong army) until breathe entered their body. We need God to breath into our lives, circumstances and situations to reveal the miracles that are in it. Alot of times, we limit who God is. But surely if He can breath into dust or a valley of bones and cause them to talk, walk and lead, He can do the same to any circumstance in your life. We have to learn how to take God out of the box and expect Him to do as He pleases. Trusting God gives you vision to discover opportunities hidden in challenges. So with challenges that we face, we must learn to pray to God over them. The prayer shouldn't always be, "Lord, take it away!" Today we will pray, "Lord, breathe on my situation and show me the miracle within!" David knew God but witnessed the manifestation of God on another level in Psalm 23 when he walked through the valley of the shadow of death. In that tragic place, God prepared a table for David in the presence of David's enemies and anointed his head with oil. Shadrach, Meshach and Abednego knew God, but witnessed the manifestation of God on another level in Daniel 3, when they refused to bow down to another God and were thrown into a fiery furnace because of it. In that tragic place, God showed up IN the fiery furnace with them. They were released without a burn or the smell of smoke in their clothes. Paul and Silas knew God but witnessed the manifestation of God on another level in Acts 16. They were put in prison for doing the work of Christ and when their praises to God went up, He showed up. The prison doors were miraculously opened. David, the 3 Hebrew boys, and Paul and Silas were faced with challenging situations but miracles were created through them. Many people missed Jesus' entry into the world because he didn't come in the package expected. As you're personally being revived in these 30 days, it's very important that you fix your eyes on the new insight and directions God will reveal in challenges. No longer will you allow what you see to hinder what you believe! Miracles are taking place. Opportunities are presenting themselves and just because they're not coming in ways that you expect it, does not mean you have to miss them.

Scripture: {Psalms 33:6 Nkjv} By the word of the LORD the heavens were made, And by the breath of His mouth all their host.

Prayer: *Dear God, You are my life. You have breathed into me the breath of life, and I have become a living being. In you I live and move and have my being.) I acknowledge You are the God of the impossible. You can do anything. I trust in Your ability not my own. Teach me to see difficulties in my life from Your perspective. Help me to focus on You and Your power. Help me not to fear but to trust You in all situations. I declare my faith in Your ability to fulfill Your promises to me. Allow Your breath that reveals miracles to consume my circumstances & situations. Allow your breath to give me strength and help me to be courageous in everything you put before me. I will not be terrified or discouraged, for You will be with me wherever I go. You know the best plan for my life. I will not focus on oppositions or challenges but trust in what you're doing through for me through them. Reveal Your supernatural power. Teach me how to continue to walk by faith.*

DAY 18

"REVEAL"

Help me to recognize the situations that I try to change are situations you're using to change me for the better. Reveal the power that I have to create change! Reveal the power of my change.

We've been taught to believe that discomfort or dissatisfaction is a bad thing. We believe we should do everything possible to avoid it. Very rarely do we consider God might be using things to make us uncomfortable so we'll do something more. If you take a fish out of water and sit it on dry land it would be uncomfortable and eventually die. Fish were created for water, not land. Its purpose is in water. A lot of times we're stagnated in a place because we don't fully understand our purpose so we don't live in our purpose. We refuse to be effect in who we are. We find it hard to stay in our own lane. God will use discomfort to get us back in His will or to push us along in His will. I remember it was time for me to leave my former church. I loved that church so much. I was so comfortable with the way things were going for my life in that church. When it was time for me to go, I was fearful and fought against God's will for me to move on. I tried to explain to God often why I was supposed to stay at that church. I wasn't ready to come out of my comfort zone. I wasn't ready for the change. My purpose was in the church but God was calling me to Pastor my own. That phase of my life was complete and it was time for me to shift. God had more people for me to reach. I was unable to reach them because I was out of place. God made things uncomfortable for me and I now understand it was God's way of moving me along. Though things were going well in my life and the church was an awesome church, God was simply saying, "You got all that you needed from this place. There's another dimension of who you are in your next move." God began to reveal to me what the power my obedience consisted of. Our purpose is not about us. It's about what God wants to do through you! He called you to a purpose and wants you to walk in it! I remember when God laid a new ministry for women on my heart. I was excited and moved forward. It was successful but the time came when God was requiring more of me so the ministry could go to another level. Another level meant more time, more exposure and more accountability. I didn't feel I was ready. I again fought against the change and God made things uncomfortable. When it was said and done, I submitted to the growth and the benefit was marvelous. We don't always know how great our purpose is so we don't always reach our potential. When we pray today, we want God to reveal the greatness of who we are through Him. We want Him to reveal to us why the change is necessary and the power behind it. We no longer want to make certain situations be change for our liking but we want God to reveal to us how this certain situations make us better and effective. Take note of situations that you are attempting to change and God is using it to change you! Change isn't always easy but when God calls for a change, you reap the benefits. The power that's in you is the power the world needs.

Scripture: {Jeremiah 29:11 Niv} For I know the plans I have for you, declares the LORD, "plans to prosper you and not to harm you, plans to give you hope and a future."

Prayer: Heavenly Father, thank you for Your plans for my life. Thank You for Your plans to bring prosperity to my life. The adversity strengthens and builds character in me so that I can walk into my purpose with readiness. Make your will clear to me and show me Your path. Reveal the greatness of who I am through You. I humble myself at Your feet not only to hear You Lord but to respond. Respond to Your call with obedience. Teach me how to be patient when You don't speak and how to move in obedience when You instruct me to move. Grant me a willing heart to obey everything that You will speak. Bind the hand of the enemy from bringing confusion and loose clarity to walk in the prosperously, purpose and the plans you have for me. Give me grace to receive and do what You plan for my life concerning my health, my family, my ministry & my finances.

DAY 19

"LEAD MY SEED"

Speak to my hands today. Show me where my seeds need to be planted. Reveal to me the good ground. Open up doors & windows that give me the opportunity to sow into someone else's need.

Sowing seed brings you harvest. The key to you receiving your harvest is where you sow your seed. If you sow in rocky places or among thorns your harvest will be empty. But if you sow amongst good soil, which produces a crop, your harvest will be multiplied. God gives seed to the sower and the sower often meets the needs of others. You ought to expect God to multiply your seed. If you're anything like me, you find joy in sowing seeds. Not only because you reap from sowing but the joy of seeing others benefit from seeds that you've sown. If it's better to give than receive, then why wouldn't we want God to lead our seed?! Giving is not a debt you owe, it's a seed you sow. The size of the seed is not the issue...the soil in which you choose to plant your seed makes the difference! If you are doing things God's way; giving generously and with the right motivation, then you can expect God to meet your needs and lead your seed. God wants you to prosper financially (and in all areas of your life) but we must follow in obeying our giving. It unleashes God's supernatural provision. Whatever you sow in life, you're going to reap. Whatever you deposit (and some) is going to be returned to you. You don't just reap what you sow. You always reap *more* than you sow! You become more like God who is a giver. On today, my desire was for my seed to land in the right place where it was most effective. I asked God for more money (seed) so I could bless others. 2 Corinthians 9:6 teaches us that sowers will be enriched in every way for great generosity. We receive an even greater ability to be generous. The more you give, the more you will be able to give

Scripture: {2 Corinthians 9:8-13 Erv} And God can give you more blessings than you need, and you will always have plenty of everything. You will have enough to give to every good work. As the Scriptures say, "He gives generously to the poor; his goodness will continue forever." God is the one who gives seed to those who plant, and he gives bread for food. And God will give you spiritual seed and make that seed grow. He will produce a great harvest from your goodness. God will make you rich in every way so that you can always give freely. And you're giving through us will make people give thanks to God. The service you are offering helps God's people with their needs, but that is not all it does. It is also bringing more and more thanks to God. This service is a proof of your faith, and people will praise God

***Prayer:** Dear Lord, please help me to know where to sow my seed. Help me to sow it by faith, confidently expecting it to meet the needs of someone else. I am a giver and therefore a receiver of Your promised blessings. Father, I thank You for leading my seed. I thank You in advance for the abundance that will flow through my life. Every need will be met, there will be no lack. Prepare the ground for my seed. My seed* *shall give to others and bring back a harvest of increase, favor, overflow & prosperity!*

DAY 20

"SHOW MERCY"

Forgive me if I've offended any of your children. Open my eyes to where I've done wrong to others and lead me in righting the wrong. Have mercy on me and give strength and compassion to the offended and hurt. Help me not to expect forgiveness but to seek it.

God is known to be a God of mercy and grace. God is merciful to even the worst offenders, sinners, and lawbreakers. This means that even though He knows of our guilt, He doesn't always issue the punishment deserved. But because He is merciful doesn't mean we get off free. Offending someone seems rather easy. We probably have all offended or hurt someone's feelings, whether it was intentional or not. We offend by our selfishness and lack of consideration of others. Some of us lack empathy, the ability to put ourselves in another's shoes, and so we offend others. In Matthew 25, there's a story about the King who invites the sheep into His Kingdom to receive blessings. He told them they were invited because when He was hungry they fed Him. When He was in prison they came to visit Him. When He had no clothes they clothed Him. When He had no place to stay they gave him a room. When He was thirsty they gave Him drink and when He was sick they took care of Him. The sheep had no idea what the King was talking about and they told Him they didn't remember doing this for Him. Ahhh...but He told them, "When you did this for the least, you did it for Me!" God pays attention to what we do. It's like doing it unto Him. So when we wrongly offend or hurt one another, we do this unto God. God is very clear about causing someone to stumble or bringing offense to others; He doesn't like it. As I traveled this journey of Revival, the goal was to become restored and renewed in God. Restoration requires a cleansing. Today we swallow any pride or justification that we're holding on to. Remembering God holds us accountable for our actions. Parents, if anyone has offended your child, you'd have an issue right? Spouses, if anyone offended your better half you'd have an issue right? Family and Friends, if someone offended someone you loved, you'd have an issue right? So does God. We want God to be merciful to us because of what we've done but we also want God to heal the heart of those we've offended. Yes, we know as Christian we are to forgive so it should be expected but be mindful that hurt can be painful. It can cause one to build walls and isolate themselves. So instead of expecting we should seek (ask) for forgiveness from anyone we've offended. Ask God to show you if you've offended anyone and you may not know you've done it. Don't be blinded by justification. Pray your eyes are opened to "the right thing to do unto God" having patience and compassion while the offended one heals!

Scripture: {Matthew 5:23-24 Niv} "Therefore if you are presenting your offering at the altar, and there remember that your brother has something against you, leave your offering and go; first be reconciled to your brother, and then come and present your offering"

Prayer: *Heavenly Father, my savior! You have commanded me to love others as myself. If I have offended anyone forgive me. Deliver me from any area of my life where I feel justified for offending others. I ask to be forgiven for whatever I may have said, done or even thought that has caused hurt to others. Allow conviction to always be my portion when I've wronged others. Touch the heart of those I've offended. Present opportunities to right any wrong. Give those I've offended the strength and mind to receive my forgiveness. Restore their trust, confidence, peace and heart. Lord, forgive me. As I offended others, I've sinned against you.*

DAY 21

"SURRENDER"

I desire to renew the covenant! Show me every area where I've voided it and take me back. I come with my mind and heart open and hands lifted. Take me back to the heart of worship, where it's all about you! The place where faith was the floor I confidently stood on and you were the one I worked hard to please.

We are creatures of habit. If we don't find ways to remind ourselves why we do what we do, we're prone to just go through the motions, or even adopt some new underlying motivation altogether. Which can be especially dangerous in our worship to God. The heart of worship is our heart, delighting in Jesus and the things the Scriptures teach us about who he is and what he has done for us on the cross. It is "all about" Jesus, not us. It involves us, but it's all about Him. He's at the center. He's the focus. It's his commands we consider first, not our preferences. Many of us have an addiction to being busy, to activity. The problem with that is our activity often keeps us from communing with God and prevents us from true worship. When He died on the cross there was a blood covenant made between us. Jesus shed His blood so that we could be redeemed and be reconciled back to God. This is surely enough for us to worship Him with our lives. Worship is not the slow song that the choir sings. Worship is not the amount you place in the offering basket. Worship is not volunteering at church. Yes, these may be acts or expressions of worship, but they do not define what true worship is. Worship is to honor with love and submission to God. Worship isn't something we simply feel. If we relegate worship to a once a week activity of singing and fellowship, then we have missed the bigger picture of what worship really is. Worship is about honoring God in everything we do. We worship God whenever we perform an act of desire to draw attention to His greatness. One portion of His greatness was revealed in the Blood covenant He made with us; sending His son as a sacrifice for our sins. God has given us so much. Only a life of continual worship (and praise) can honor God's numerous gifts to us. A worshipper keeps God first in all things! A worshipper is living a life trying to please God in all that they do! What God thinks matters! What God sees matters! We must often be reminded that we owe God our lives! Worship is a response to God for all that He has given to our lives. True worship, in other words, is defined by the priority we place on who God is in our lives and where God is on our list of priorities. True worship is a matter of the heart expressed through a lifestyle of holiness. This means every moment is the right time to worship. Remind yourself what the blood shed on the cross was all about...now LOVE on God with your life of obedience, faith, trust and worship! Jesus is greatly honored when we bring ourselves, with the Holy Spirit's help, back to the heart of worship again and again.

Scripture: {2 Samuel 7:22 Niv} How great you are, Sovereign Lord! There is no one like you, and there is no God but you, as we have heard with our own ears.

Prayer: Lord, I know You didn't have to do it, but You did! Thank You for the bloodshed that reconciled me back to You. That gave me grace and mercy so I'm able to truly worship You. Thank You! I've allowed things (list personal things) in life to cause me to lose sight of what true worship it. I continue to surrender my will to Yours, my ways to Yours, my thoughts to Yours. Lord, renew my mind back to the cross! Because of the bloodshed, my life belongs to You! Because of the bloodshed you belong to me! Continue drawing my heart to You. Guide my mind; fill my imagination that I may be wholly yours, dedicated to you!

DAY 22

"YOUR PERSONAL DAY"

Worry is wasting energy on the things you can't control. Leave everything in God's hand. Think less, pray more!

Release everything today! Though you've been praying for the last 21 days, I'm sure there is something you haven't touched on. I'm sure there is something the enemy keeps poking at you about! OF COURSE HE IS! You're almost there...PERSONAL REVIVAL! He wants you to believe it's all in vain. He wants to keep reminding you of what "hasn't" taken place yet! Today I want you to pray however you feel or are led. FREE your mind today of anything that has been trying to linger on and hinder you. Whether it be the children, your spouse, coworker, your house, your job, just give it to God today!!

Scripture: {Proverbs 3:5-6 Nkjv} Trust in the Lord with all your heart, And lean not on your own understanding; **in** all your ways acknowledge Him, And He shall direct your paths.

Prayer: Dear Heavenly Father, (you finish the rest! Take what you've prayed thus far and bring it all together! LET GO & LET GOD!)

DAY 23

POSITION ME

Psalm 1:1 "Blessed is the man that WALKS not in the counsel of the ungodly, nor STANDS in the path of sinners, nor SITS in the seat of the scornful."

Ahhh...POSITION, POSITION, POSITION

Everybody wants to be blessed! I know I sure do! I've learned through the Word, your position, positions you for blessing! There is a way we ought not to walk, a path we will not stand in, and a seat we will not sit in. The path and lifestyle of the blessed man is not with those who are distant from God. The way of the world is tempting and alluring. It can sometimes be appealing. It's a way of pleasure and sometimes acceptance with others. But the blessed man doesn't position his life by this way. There's always the danger that the walk we think is going to be a walk with the Lord will turn into another kind of walk. I often have seen many start off great in God. The desire was for Him. The passion was for Him. The glory was always given to Him. But influence caused their walk to sway from the ways of the Lord. Though that isn't fully my story, there were times where I just wasn't as enthused about Pastoring like I was when I first started. There were times when things, situations and even people influenced my thoughts. My thoughts caused me to walk, stand and even sit differently than I started out with God. I'm sure your testimony has some similarities. We've all had moments where we just wanted to "be ourselves" and "do our own thing." We've all had moments where we "set our minds on earthly things" instead of heavenly things like Colossians 3:2 teaches us. We found that our value systems, rather than being shaped by the Word of God, were actually values that we picked up from our culture, the media, our friends or even our generational background. In order to remain blessed we have to learn how to stay in position. When you are wrongly positioned, the plans and purpose of God for your life will not be fulfilled. It's important that we examine ourselves in accordance with God's word to make sure we're properly positioned for His blessings. Reading Psalm 1 brings much light to the importance of position. When we walk in the counsel (guidance and direction) of the ungodly, we walk in the direction of their influence! Keep in mind, this could be social media, television shows, world systems, friends and family. Through prayer today, eliminate the counsel of the ungodly you knowingly or unknowingly walk in. When we stand in the ways of a sinner, we come in agreement with them. Through prayer today, eliminate any stance you may have taken with the sinner and his sinful ways. Again, knowingly and unknowingly. When we sit in the seat of the scorner, we become complacent and comfortable with them who mock God and His ways. Our prayer today will be for God to restore proper influence so our lives are positioned for blessings!

Scripture: {1 Corinthians 15:33 Niv} Bad company corrupts good character.

Prayer: *Lord, do whatever is necessary to KEEP me in position! I chose to operate by Your Spirit of Wisdom. My mind is focused on You, Lord, and the truth of Your Word. My ear is tuned to hear Your words of counsel. I seek Your instruction which is true and life-giving. I chose to have You give direction to my life. Eliminate all that have taken the place of your influence. My desire to be like a tree planted besides sure water. Nourish and refresh my ears and eyes! And I thank You in advance for prospering my life through your ways.*

DAY 24

PREPARED

I've moved from expecting the promise to entering my position! God made me some promises! They've awaited my arrival. I was positioned in favor! I was positioned in deliverance! I was positioned in my healing! I am prepared for the breakthrough! I'm not getting ready! I'm ready! I've been PREPARED for this place that God promised! LET'S GO!

How do you feel when you stand on the verge of reaching an awaited goal? Are you happy or relieved that the journey is nearly over? Are you frightened of the tests and trials that may still lie ahead, or do you view your future with courage and faith in God? If you have made efforts to stay the course during this 30 day journey, then you must take note of things that have changed in your life during this time. Something has shifted! Whatever that something is, I'm sure in the beginning you weren't too confident that it would be obtained. You knew you needed a push, a pull, motivation, support or even a strategy; if not you wouldn't have started this 30 day journey but I'm sure something in the back of your mind at least once said, "what if this 30 day journey is pointless?" I know I did, quite a few times. Think about the children of Israel as they were traveling through the wilderness to the "Promised Land." There were times they thought, "We should turn back. This journey is too hard. This journey is pointless. This can't be the will of God because we've had to endure too much," and when they finally made it to the Promised Land, they were afraid to enter. Because of what they saw. The land that God promised them was occupied by giants and they didn't think they could conquer it. When the Israelites came out of the wilderness, they had to seize the land. Our promised land is where we can live out the promises of God. It is a place where the promises of God are experienced in all their fullness. Today I want you to look back 23 days ago and take note of your progression. Don't look at how small, just acknowledge the progress. Don't pay too much attention to how many days you have left. Just acknowledge how much you've progressed thus far. If nothing else, you've increased your commitment to pray. You've seen God manifest things you've only "thought" of or just "heard" about. You've gained more knowledge and revelation of who He is and who you are through Him. The place you are today, awaited your arrival. Long before the children of Israel left their place of bondage (Egypt) God promised them freedom and prosperity; a land flowing with milk & honey! It took them 40 years for their release but God kept His promise! What He promised awaited their arrival! They entered the Promised Land but not without a fight! As they stood on the mountaintop overlooking the Promised Land they should have stood in confidence. Ready to pursue what God promised them. Even after seeing the giants who occupied THEIR land, they should have recognized the God who parted the Red Sea to save them from their enemies. The God who swallowed up their enemies with that same Red Sea. The God who fed them with food (manna) from Heaven when they had no food.

The God who led them at night by fire and in the day by a cloud would surely bring them through this! Joshua even said to some of them in Joshua 18:3, "How long will you neglect to go and possess the land which the Lord God of your fathers has given you?" God already prepared them in the wilderness! He's trustworthy and faithful and He's a promise keeper. The adversary is still occupying some things God promised you but you have what it takes to conquer it! God prepared you...Now go get it in faith and confidence!

Scripture: {1 Peter 5:10 Esv} And after you have suffered a little while, the God of all grace, who has called you to his eternal glory in Christ, will himself restore, confirm, strengthen, and establish you.

***Prayer:** Dear Lord, today, I receive my FULL inheritance. I receive by faith EVERYTHING that rightfully belongs to me through Jesus' sacrifice. I receive my FULL inheritance based on being an heir of You. I claim it ALL. Thank you for supernatural strength and resolve as I enter new territories. I'm leaning on You and You alone as I conquer my land and possess the territory (list some promises that God made to you) that You have promised me. I stand in confidence against all that is a hindrance to my possession of my promises (list things that hinder you. Example: fear, complacency, doubt, discouragement, etc.) I believe all things are possible through you and I thank you for preparing me for my next place of promise!*

DAY 25

NO REQUEST - THANKFUL FOR GRACE & MERCY

There are times I forget to be thankful. Times when circumstances and all that is simply life seem to get in the way of being able to clearly see my life for what it is. To see all the beauty found in all the little things. All the big things and all those in between. Life is full of blessings. Full of grace; receiving what we do not deserve from God. Full of mercy; not receiving the punishment from God that we deserve. And I must choose to see it.

Take time today and just be thankful! Your life if full of blessings! Speak of your appreciation for what God has done/doing and who He has been/being to you! Life would be worthless and meaningless without the grace, mercy and love of God. When was the last time you told God you love and appreciate Him? Regardless of how long or short time ago it was, today is still the perfect time to let Him know how precious His mercy is to you and how liberating His grace is for you!

Scripture: {Psalm 63:3} Because Your loving-kindness *is* better than life, My lips shall praise You.

Prayer: *Loving Father, forgive me for times, I've neglected to say thank you! Thank You, Lord for the best gift ever given in Christ Jesus that He would die on a cross, in the place of my sins. I do not have adequate words to express my thanks, my* *appreciation, and most importantly, my love for you. But please receive my words knowing the commitment and passion of my heart when I say, "Dear God, I love you." Thank you for loving me unconditionally. Without you, I'd be incomplete. Thank you for Your mercy and Your grace! Thank you for your blessings, protection and favor that was so undeserving. In spite what I may have experienced, thank You for being in control. Lord, I don't deserve all that You have done in my life, but thank You for being so kind. Thank You for the gift of the Holy Spirit, who leads and guides me in truth. I'm grateful, your mercy is amazing, and your grace never ends. This is the day that you have made; I will rejoice and be glad in it! Thank You!*

DAY 26

SERPENT WISDOM

We need the same wisdom Satan operated in at the Garden of Eden. (Genesis 3) When attempting to cause mankind to fall, he was wise enough to know who to go to; the vulnerable vessel, the woman, Eve. He knew what to say and when to say it. Satan had a plan to fulfill. He used strategy and wisdom to complete his mission. Matthew 10:16 says Jesus was sending His disciples out into the world. He was sending them into dangerous territory and He told them, "I send you out like sheep among the wolves." The wolf is a terrible beast of prey, known for its appetite, cunning, and fierceness. Sheep, on the other hand, are weak and witless; surely no match for the strength and craftiness of a wolf. In the presence of wolves, sheep are in great danger because they have in themselves no effective means of defense. When the disciple went out in the world to preach the gospel they would be in great danger. The mission of sharing the gospel would be opposed. Jesus instructed them to be wise as serpents. He wanted them to be smart about how they conducted themselves. Jesus was saying, be smart, be aware of what is going on. So we must operate in wisdom! Kingdom work takes wisdom. As we bring the gospel to a hostile world, whether it be through the preached word or the exemplifying of our lives, we must avoid the snares of the enemy that is set before us. Of course we're not supposed to deceive. Taking on the wisdom of a serpent does not include taking on the character of one! But we definitely should model some of the serpent's shrewdness but in a positive manner. It's important to know how to be on guard against snares, traps and deceptions that will be thrown your way in order to knock you off course and keep you off course. Being wise is to have sharp and perceptive discernment and understanding. Being wise gives you the ability to perceive and escape danger. Serpents are known for their cleverness and craftiness in the Bible. In the specific context of Matthew 10, the cunning trait of snakes is what enabled the 12 disciples to continue to survive while preaching and teaching to a world that hated them for what they stood for: Jesus Christ. The point is...be smart! As you continue on this journey of "reviving" yourself, you want to be ready to bring life to someone else. Soul winning is our responsibility and you must pray for the same wisdom Jesus was instructing His disciple to have when He was sending them out into the world. We have a responsibility to win souls. Remember, there will be opposition but YOU CAN DO IT! Proverbs 11:30 "...he that win souls is WISE!"

Scripture: {Proverbs 4:6-7 Erv} Don't turn away from wisdom, and she will protect you. Love her, and she will keep you safe. The first step to becoming wise is to look for wisdom, so use everything you have to get understanding.

Prayer: *Lord, grant me wisdom to accomplish what You have put before me with grace and humility and solely for Your glory. Give me wisdom to discern between good and evil in all that is around me and all that is within me. Give me wisdom to love others as You do; to understand their value and to accept them* *unconditionally. May You grant me wisdom to treasure Your many blessings; all that You have given me and all that You have shown me. Give me the wisdom that comes from above*

DAY 27

HUMILITY

If we want to be effective, we must learn to walk in the humility of Jesus.

Imagine if you were God, equal with the Father, sharing glory with Him, having every privilege of being God and then you become a man and laid aside all those privileges. *"He is the image of the invisible God"* (Colossians 1:15). We must embrace this most important lesson and learn to clothe ourselves in this noble garment of humility. Jesus never fails to show us that the way of God's Kingdom comes through humility. Jesus showed us His core identity when He took off His robe and girded Himself with a towel and washed His disciple's feet (John 13). He also revealed His humility when He, the King, entered Jerusalem riding on a donkey, a small lowly animal yet, He was revealing the nature of His kingship (Matthew 21). They admired Jesus but didn't understand why He rode a donkey. Jesus was entering a failing kingdom riding on a symbol of humility. Today we'll pray that we too embrace or continue to embrace the same nature of humility as Jesus. It can sometimes be difficult to be humble when you have achieved so much. Whether we have achieved much or not, humility is difficult for all of us, but it remains the key. Being humble for most people brings to mind a form of weakness. God calls us to humble ourselves under Him. Not because He is controlling and just simply wants us to bow to Him because we're nothing, but rather because He wants to exalt us and care for us. As we humble ourselves, that is when we truly worship Him. We're trusting Him with what's going on in our lives and believing He is the provider instead of ourselves. Humility is the key to being able to listen and find joyful rewards. Pride, on the other hand, causes one to be spiritually deaf and ultimately to stumble into destruction. Ezekiel 28:17 describes Lucifer's problem and why he was cast out of Heaven. Lucifer thought he "had it all." His heart was proud because of his beauty. Pride led a revolt in Heaven before time and history as we know it. Pride remains first among the things that God hates even now (Proverbs 6:17). There was no room for pride in heaven then and there isn't any room for it on earth now. Pride promises so much but lands us right in disaster and destruction. Pride ushers to fall. Pride uses our resources, gifts, and successes to blind us to the fact that it is all by God's grace. It blinds us to His counsel and to our own weaknesses. Pride makes us deaf and blind to truth. Humility as you are doing great things keeps you on top but always at the footstool of God. Jesus would have us to wear the grace of humility in our hearts. (Matthew 11:29) therefore He says, "Learn of me; for I am meek and lowly in heart."

Scripture: {1 Peter 5:6-7 Esv} Humble yourselves, therefore, under the mighty hand of God so that at the proper time He may exalt you, casting all your anxieties on Him, because He cares for you."

Prayer: Dear Lord, who, by your example, instructed me to be meek and humble, give me grace, in every thought, word, and action, to imitate your meekness and humility. Continue to show me that I am never to seek my own glory, but always look unto you. Restrain my thoughts, so that they do not wander to the vanities of this world. I desire my actions, thoughts and words to be worship unto you. All Glory belongs to you. Sow in me the seed of humility; and keep me under the wings of your grace. Hide me through your mercy. Keep me from falling prey to the many temptations that pride seems to scatter in my path, where I want to be the center of attention and desire to receive all the acclaim and the glory that rightly belongs to You. Teach me Your ways and show me how I may clothe myself in humility towards others. Thank You for opening up Your Word to me and helping me to see the beautiful truth about humility!

DAY 28

FASTING & MEDITATING

Through studying His Word, God introduces Himself so you can understand His character. But we must respond to Him through prayer, fasting and meditation, especially focusing on how we will relate to Him. David, who was identified as "a man after God's own heart" (Acts 13:22) came to know God through his prayer, fasting and meditation. Likewise, as we grow in our relationship with God we can come to identify with David. Prayer, fasting and meditation are three essential factors for building a real relationship with God. We've been tackling prayer for the last 27 days. When you learn to incorporate fasting and meditation, it takes your growth to another level. Fasting and meditation should become a part of your identity. It shouldn't be done only when adversity comes. By the time adversity shows up, because of your consistent fasting and meditating on God's Word, you really won't be moved and you're prepared to overcome. In Mark 9, the disciples were unsuccessful with casting a demon out of a boy. They asked Jesus, "Why couldn't we cast them out?" Jesus then told them, "This kind only comes out through fasting and prayer." This didn't mean they were supposed to let the boy go and start fasting and praying. Jesus was clearly telling them you must have a lifestyle of fasting and prayer. Jesus was teaching a principle here. Some things will only obey a disciplined disciple.

Meditating on the Word is so important! We must read it daily and meditate on it daily. In His Word you find provision and understanding. God told Joshua in Joshua 1:8 "Keep the word always on your lips, meditating on it that you're careful to do what is written." It sets us up for prosperity and success. We hold in our hands the key to success in every area of our lives, through the Word of God! When meditating on the Word we must process (study it), proclaim (declare it) and practice it (keeping doing it).

Fasting is just as important as prayer and meditation. It involves laying aside our human strength to move in supernatural strength. Fasting *generally* refers to a period of abstinence from food for the purpose of engaging in uninterrupted study, prayer and meditation with a clear objective and goal in focus. As Christians, fasting is one of the Godly exercises we should engage in regularly. The advantages are numerous. Through fasting, we can improve our effectiveness in the things of the Spirit. Fasting helps you to tame the flesh and lift the spirit. We are required to walk in the Spirit always. This means to be spirit led and not flesh led. Fasting and meditation helps to sharpen our ability to receive or hear from God. It can be a vehicle to change things that pertain to us or even in the circumstances of others around us. It is important to know that fasting is not an effort to change God. Fasting does not put pressure on God. When we fast, we are the ones that change and we are the beneficiaries of the fast. When fasting, have a clear objective in focus. Having a clear focus and expectation will help guide your prayers. Our period of fasting must include regular intervals of prayer, study and *meditation* on the Word. Fasting and meditating on God's word keeps us in tune with God during prayer. Fasting causes the flesh to be weak. Meditating on the Word causes our spirit man to be strong. So when we enter into prayer with a weak flesh and a strong spirit, we're in a place to speak and pray according to God's Word and able to hear God clearly. Before any time of fasting that is planned, prepare your mind, heart and body. Choose what you will fast from. Prepare how you will do it. Inform those who need to know, for example: spouse and family.

Scripture: Nehemiah 9:1-3, "On the twenty-fourth day of the same month, the Israelites gathered together, fasting and wearing sackcloth and putting dust on their heads. Those of Israelite descent had separated themselves from all foreigners. They stood in their places and confessed their sins and the sins of their ancestors. They stood where they were and read from the Book of the Law of the Lord their God for a quarter of the day, and spent another quarter in confession and in worshiping the Lord their God."

***Prayer:** Jesus, my desire is to be disciplined. My desire is to draw closer to you in fasting, prayer and meditation. Give me the grace to fast consistently and the strength to fast when you require. My desire is to honor you through fasting and meditating on your Word. I don't want anything to separate me from you. Help me to walk by the Word. Give me understanding and clarity of Your Word pertaining to my life. Keep me from being distracted by my wants, my desires and my thoughts that hinder me from your will. As my flesh becomes weak, Lord give me the strength of Your might, to focus, to hold on and to fight.*

DAY 29

ENDURANCE

This 30 Day Journey is coming to an end. It's been rough and fulfilling. The enemy fought you, you fought you and God continued to fight for you! You endured and must continue enduring. After these 30 days, your life should be revived. You should be encouraged and empowered but never be ignorant to Satan's continued devices. There will always be greater for you. There will always be better for you. There will always be more required. Luke 12:48 "...For everyone to whom much is given, from him much will be required; and to whom much has been committed, of him they will ask the more." The idea of "to whom much is given, much will be required" is that we are held responsible for what we have. If we are blessed with talents, wealth, knowledge, time, and the like, it is expected that we use these well to glorify God and benefit others. God has gifted and anointed you with a lot and of course Satan will fight against it. You should have learned thus far, you have enduring traits! Every day we will face challenges. They will come in many forms; physical, financial difficulties, emotional and even faith struggles but you must keep going back to things you know to be true: God's Word. Don't doubt in the dark what you have already seen in the light. Rely on the sources God has given you: HIS POWER (Luke 10:19), HIS GRACE (2 Corinthians 12:9) and HIS LOVE (John 3:16-17). Don't allow circumstance or situations to push you backwards.

Keep pressing toward the mark of the HIGH CALLING which is Jesus Christ!

Scripture: {Matthew 24:13 Nkjv} But he who endures until the end shall be saved.

Prayer: *Father, I thank You for a brand new day with new opportunities, challenges and mercy. Help me not to function in my own strength, but in the power of the Holy Spirit. May I stand firm in the truth of the gospel and remain steadfastly looking to Jesus - trusting in Him to supply His sufficient strength. Give me the courage and strength to press on toward in Christ Jesus. Strengthen and uphold me in the power of Your Spirit, and to sustain and comfort me I pray, so that in all things I may patiently endure to the end.*

DAY 30

PRAISE - IT'S ALWAYS IN ORDER

You have made it! This is another opportunity to give God PRAISE!!

It's been 30 days! Take a look at who you were before you started this journey and who you are now. Take some time and reflect on the last 29 days of your life and see how things have accelerated! Now embrace the new you! See...there are benefits to consistent prayer. What you started out with (hindrances, junk, uncleanness, confusion, slothfulness, complacency) you no longer have and what you needed to have...RESTORATION IS YOUR PORTION! Praising God is useful and favorable for us. By praising God, we are reminded of the greatness of God! His power and presence in our lives is reinforced in our understanding. Praise releases strength in faith, which causes God to move in your life. God inhabits the atmosphere of praise. If we want to see a clear manifestation of God's blessings and grace, all we need to do is to praise Him with all our heart.

Scripture: {Psalm 63:3-8 Kjv} "Because Your lovingkindness is better than life, my lips shall praise You. Thus I will bless You while I live; I will lift up my hands in Your name. My soul shall be satisfied as with marrow and fatness, and my mouth shall praise You with joyful lips."

Prayer: *Let this day of prayer simply be praise! Sing, Dance, Thank! Rejoice, because He is better than great! He is a Reviver!*

www.ingramcontent.com/pod-product-compliance
Lightning Source LLC
Chambersburg PA
CBHW032127090426
42743CB00007B/498